The Night Dream

A Journal

≡Bluestreak
BOOKS

⊒Bluestreak

An imprint of Weldon Owen
1045 Sansome Street, Suite 100, San Francisco, CA 94111
www.weldonowen.com
Weldon Owen is a division of Bonnier Publishing USA

Library of Congress Cataloging in Publication data is available.

ISBN: 978-1-681-88232-1
First Printed in 2017
10 9 8 7 6 5 4 3 2 1
Printed in China

Developed by The Book Shop, Ltd.
Designer   Eleanor Kwei

This Journal Belongs To:

A dream that is not understood is like a letter not opened.

The Talmud

Dreams are faithful interpreters of our inclinations; but there is art required to sort and understand them.

Montaigne

Dreams are a drama taking place on one's own interior stage.

Carl Jung

I've always had access to other worlds. We all do because
we all dream.

Leonora Carrington

The spirit of man has two dwelling places: both this world and the other world. The borderland between them is the third, the land of dreams.

Bruhad Aranyaka

It is not our idleness, in our dreams, that the submerged truth sometimes comes to the top.

Virginia Woolf

Dreams are an involuntary kind of poetry.

Jean Paul Richter

I'll let you be in my dreams if I can be in yours.

Bob Dylan

Dreams are true while they last and do we not live in dreams?

Alfred, Lord Tennyson

Trust in dreams, for in them is hidden the gate of eternity.

Kahlil Gibran

You see things; and you say, 'Why?' But I dream things that never were; and I say, 'Why not?'"

George Bernard Shaw

People who are most afraid of their dreams convince themselves
they don't dream at all.

John Steinbeck

All men whilst they are awake are in one common world: but each of them, when he is asleep, is in a world of his own.

Plutarch

Huge and mighty forms that do not live like living men, moved slowly through the mind by day and were trouble to my dreams.

William Wordsworth

In dreams we catch glimpses of a life larger than our own.

Helen Keller

What would an ocean be without a monster lurking in the dark?
It would be like sleep without dreams.

Werner Herzog

You eat, in dreams, the custard of the day.

Alexandar Pope

To all, to each, a fair good-night,
And pleasing dreams, and slumbers light!

Sir Walter Scott

For in that sleep of death what dreams may come.

William Shakespeare

A sweet thing, for whatever time, to revisit in dreams the dear
dead we have lost.

Euripides

Why does the eye see a thing more clearly in dreams than the mind while awake?

Leonardo Da Vinci

Dreams are often most profound when they seem most crazy.

Sigmund Freud

It may be that those who do most, dream most.

Stephen Locke

Dreams are illustrations . . . from the book your soul is writing about you.

Marsha Norman

The dream . . . is a texture woven of time and space inside which
we find ourselves.

Robert Bosnack

We are such stuff as dreams are made on; and our little life is rounded with a sleep.

William Shakespeare

One can write, think and pray exclusively of others; dreams are all egocentric.

Evelyn Waugh

A dream that is not understood remains a mere occurrence;
understood, it becomes a living experience.

Carl Jung

I don't use drugs, my dreams are frightening enough.

M. C. Escher

Is this is a dream? O, if it be a dream,
Let me sleep on, and do not wake me yet!

Henry Wadsworth Longfellow

All the things one has forgotten scream for help in dreams.

Elias Canetti

Dreaming permits each and every one of us to be quietly and safely
insane every night of our lives.

William C Dement

Dreams come to tell us something about our
lives that we are missing.

James Redfield

In my dreams, I never have an age.

Madeleine L'Engle

The luxury of being half-asleep, exploring the fringes of psychosis in safety.

Ian McEwan

Dreams disdain fine lines and finishing touches on landscapes – they content
themselves with thick but representative brushstrokes.

Machado de Assis

Our life is composed greatly from dreams, from the unconscious, and they must be brought into connection with action. They must be woven together.

Anaïs Nin

The best reason for having dreams is that in dreams no reasons are necessary.

Ashleigh Brilliant

We are more curious about the meaning of dreams than about
things we see when awake.

Diogenes Laërtius

Judge of your natural character by what you do in your dreams.

Ralph Waldo Emerson

In dreams it is often the case that the greatest extravagances
seem bereft of their power to astonish and the most improbable
chimeras seem commonplace.

Cormac McCarthy

Dream Glossary

ABUSE

If you are the abuser in the dream, you may feel guilty about the way you are treating someone. If you are being abused in the dream, you may feel victimized by someone.

ACCIDENT

This may be a precognitive dream; be extra careful when driving or performing an activity in which accidents are more likely to occur.

ADOPTION

You may feel confused about your identity.

ADULTERY

You may have suspicions about your partner's fidelity, or you may want to act out a forbidden temptation—sexual or otherwise. According to Freud, dreams about adultery are a means by which you can safely fulfill your wishes without having to deal with the repercussions.

ADVANCEMENT

A good omen; deep down, you are aware that good fortune is coming.

AIRPLANE

If you are a passenger on an airplane, it means you feel that your life is changing. If you are watching an airplane disappear in the dream, it symbolizes that you have avoided a conflict.

ALARM

You have reason to be worried. Your unconscious is telling you a disaster could occur. (Or maybe your alarm clock is going off!)

ALLEY

You feel as if you are lost, or that your path in life lacks focus. However, if the alley is lit, it means that you have found a unique way of accomplishing things in your life.

ALMANAC

You may be preoccupied with meaningless details in your life.

AMBULANCE

Be wary—ambulances with sirens are bad omens. If you are on board the ambulance, it could mean you will suffer an accident or serious illness.

AMUSEMENT PARK

Pleasure and merriment. Either you are currently happy with your life, or you can soon expect a period of mirth.

ANCHOR

You are either seeking stability or you feel that someone or something is weighing you down. You may be in a relationship with a person who is too needy.

ANGEL

You feel safe, you trust your instincts, or you believe someone is watching over you. Enjoy this comfortable feeling.

ANTENNAE

You feel distrustful of a relationship you are in. Your unconscious is telling you that you need to examine this relationship and evaluate its effect on you. Be forewarned!

APPLES

Good health. You feel healthy, physically and/or mentally.

ARCH

Success. You are accomplishing or will accomplish a great feat.

ARROW

Fortune and pleasure. However, if the arrow is broken, you can expect difficulty and obstacles in your path.

ASHES

Failure. You may feel that you have failed at something, or that other people are failing you.

ASYLUM

Mental anguish or a feeling of being overwhelmed. It is time to re-prioritize and simplify you life.

ATTIC

Imagine that a house is the body; the attic is the head. Attics represent delusion. You believe the impossible can happen. Whatever fancy ideas you are entertaining won't manifest themselves in reality. So get back down to earth!

AUTOMOBILE

You are pursuing (or traveling toward) a goal. If the trip goes well, your aspirations will come true. If, however, you get into a car accident in the dream, it is a sign that you will probably not reach your goals.

B

BABY

An indication you may be suppressing anxieties about the ticking of your biological clock. You are ready to start a family or you feel the need to nurture someone, even if it's not your own child. It could also mean a project you are working on will soon come to fruition.

BALLOON

Like a real balloon, a balloon in a dream cannot last long. This means you are involved in something that will provide only fleeting pleasure. Beware; just as balloons pop, your hopes, dreams, and expectations may be shattered.

BAPTISM

You are seeking a change, a new beginning. Perhaps it is time to simplify your life.

BARE FEET

You feel unprepared for something that is happening or will soon happen to you; you do not have the necessary skills or tools to accomplish something you are attempting.

BARN

A barn with healthy livestock means you are enjoying or will soon enjoy prosperity. If the barn is empty, expect failure or poverty.

BASKET

An empty basket means your life is not as fulfilling as you would like it to be. But if the basket is full, you most likely find your life satisfying.

BATH

If the bath water is hot in your dream, beware of something evil lurking around th. corner. Cold bath water, however, means th. joyful news is on its way.

BATS

A bad omen; you will soon experience affliction in your life. White bats symbolize an upcoming death.

BEARD

Expect a major struggle in your life. You may have to compete for something you feel is rightfully yours.

BEES

Profit. Expect increased earnings or professional advancement.

BEGGAR

If you are the beggar, you are feeling as if you will lose everything you value. You must better manage your finances or other areas of your life. On the other hand, if someone is begging from you in the dream, you feel taken advantage of. You must deal with whomever you feel is exploiting you.

BICYCLE

If you are riding a bicycle uphill, it's likely you have been working toward a goal. Riding uphill in dreams is also equated with good fortune, while riding downhill may imply that your life is spinning out of control. Riding your bike on level ground may just mean it's time to exercise.

BINOCULARS

Like antennae, binoculars mean there is someone in your life you distrust and may want to keep a closer eye on.

BIRDS

Good fortune. The more colorful the bird or lovelier its tune, the more good fortune you can expect. If a bird is killed in a dream, it is a sign of bad luck.

BOAT/RAFT

Boating in calm waters is a positive sign; there are good things in store for you. But watch out if the waters in your dream are stormy—a sign that there is trouble ahead.

BOAT'S CABIN

The cabin of a boat is generally associated with trouble. Either you are involved in a dangerous relationship or will soon meet someone who will bring misfortune into your life.

BOX

If the box is filled, you can expect good things to happen. An empty box is a sign that what you hoped for is not going to materialize.

BRIDE

A symbol of union. The union may not necessarily be marital, but will likely be long lasting.

BURGLAR

You are subconsciously aware that something of yours is being sought and may soon be taken from you. You must be vigilant if you wish to maintain what is rightfully yours.

BURIED ALIVE

This means you have made an enormous error, or are about to. Be careful in your decision-making.

BUTCHER

You feel as if your character is under scrutiny or is being picked apart; others question your honor or integrity.

BUTTERFLY

Butterflies portend the reappearance of an old friend.

BUZZARD

Scandal. You may be involved in a scandal right now and are more upset by it than you realize. Otherwise, you may soon be a victim of gossip and slander.

C

CAGE

Seeing animals trapped in a cage portends that you will win an important battle. If, however, you are the one trapped inside a cage, you may feel you are losing an important dispute.

CAKE

Satisfaction. You have been indulging yourself and quite enjoy being pampered.

CALENDAR

Keeping your life organized is of great importance to you right now.

CANAL

If the water in the canal is dirty or foul, you may expect a period of sickness. If the water is clear, you can expect good health for the next several years.

CANDLE

If the candle is burning low, it is a sign that you will soon experience a period of great confusion. Putting out a candle in your dreams indicates that you are repressing important thoughts and ideas.

CAROUSEL

Riding on a carousel indicates you are stuck in a very dull routine. However, if you are watching another person ride a carousel, it means that you are feeling envious of someone else.

CAT

Bad luck. Beware of a diabolic stranger who seeks to corrupt your world.

CEMETERY

If the cemetery is well maintained, it is likely that you will enjoy several years of good health. But if the cemetery is abandoned or unkempt, expect a period of isolation and unhappiness.

CHILD

A child in a dream often represents the dreamer as a child. You may have some unresolved issues from childhood—the rest of the dream's content will give you clues into what these unresolved issues are.

CLIMBING

The satisfying completion of a hike or climb means you feel proud of a major accomplishment. If, however, you find the climb tiresome, reconsider your expectations— you may have set unrealistic goals.

CLOWN

Happy clowns are associated with joy and merriment while sad ones generally signify defeat. Evil clowns signify deception and trickery. If you are the clown, expect to be ridiculed and mocked by others behind your back.

COFFIN

Almost always associated with death, illness, loneliness, or sorrow.

CRADLE

Rocking a baby in a cradle may seem like a beautiful image to you, but you mustn't be fooled. In fact, this may be a premonition that a close family member is seriously ill. Rocking an empty cradle is also a bad omen; you must beware of gossip and rumors that may lead to your demise.

D

DARKNESS

Indicates that you are intentionally being left out or played for a fool by people who are close to you.

DENTIST

A dentist at work often means you feel uneasy about someone or something.

DEVIL

You feel shame or despair.

DIAMONDS

Almost always an auspicious sign. If, however, the diamonds have been taken from a deceased person in the dream, your good fortune may just be a sham and you should beware.

DICTIONARY

A sign that you are too dependent on others and what they think. Take this dream as a cue to seek more autonomy and self-assurance.

DIVORCE

Indicates dissatisfaction in your marriage.

DOOR

Passing through a door means that you feel you are being stalked. Someone else passing through a door means an important endeavor of yours will fail.

DOOR KNOCKER

You are in desperate need of the advice or aid of someone close to you. A predicament you thought you could handle on your own is not as simple as you had originally believed.

DOVE

Peace. Perhaps it is time to reconcile with someone with whom you have quarreled.

DRAGON

A symbol of impending chaos. It may be time to organize your life and tie up some loose ends.

DRUM

The muffled sound of a drum is actually the call of an absent friend. Someone with whom you are close but who lives far away is in dire need of your help. To see, but not hear, a drum is an indication that you will soon reap the just rewards of your good deeds.

E

EATING

If you are dining alone, it is a sign that you are experiencing some sort of difficulty in your social relationships. If you are dining with others, your dream denotes a prosperous period in your life—either in the present or near future.

ECHO

Loneliness—others are not responding to you in a positive manner.

EGGS

Many eggs suggest great fortune. However, broken eggs portend an unsuccessful financial investment.

ELEVATOR/ESCALATOR

If you are ascending in an elevator, you will soon reach great heights in your career. However, if the elevator is descending, it is likely that you career is in a downward phase.

ENVELOPE

Unfortunately, an envelope in a dream portends misfortune. Expect to be disappointed by some news coming your way.

EXPLOSION

Stress—you are anxious about a certain aspect of your life.

EYE

You are suspicious of someone.

F

FAINTING

Strangely enough, fainting in a dream doesn't mean you should be worried about your own health. Rather, fainting often suggests that someone in your family has fallen ill.

FAIRY

A good omen—enjoy!

FALLING

If you land safely from a fall, you will prevail in a struggle. If, however, you injure yourself upon landing, it is likely that you will not achieve victory. Falling can also symbolize insecurity or a surrender to erotic temptation.

FAME

If you dream that you are famous, you will not find the success you have been anticipating. Oddly enough, if you are not the famous person in the dream, you will reach the heights you imagined.

FARM

A prosperous future.

FATHER (OR FATHER FIGURE)

A father figure in a dream may appear as a father, grandfather, or king. He may be protective, or overbearing and destructive. If you dream of being a father figure in the dream, it is a sign that you feel self-assured and in control. If someone else is the father figure, it is a sign that you feel inferior to this person.

FATIGUE

A dream in which you suffer from fatigue may be a sign that you are not well.

FIRE

Dreams of fire are much like dreams of falling. If you are not harmed by the fire, you will emerge safely from a difficult situation. However, if you are burned in the fire, you are concerned about conflicts you are facing.

FISH

Fish swimming through clear water indicate financial success. Fish swimming in murky water mean you should be cautious with your money.

FLOATING

If you are floating in clear water, you will rise above obstacles in your life. If you are floating in muddy water, you may prevail over obstacles but will not be satisfied with your success.

FLOWERS

You have or will soon have many admirers. However, if the flowers are wilted, those who used to admire you are losing interest.

FLYING

You desire freedom; you want to get out of a situation you are in.

FOREIGNER

If your encounter with a foreigner is positive, luck is on your side. A negative encounter portends misfortune.

FOUNTAIN

Clear water in a fountain indicates that an intimate relationship is pleasing. Murky water may suggest involvement in a risky love affair.

FUNERAL

Never a good omen. If you are being buried, it is likely that you are unsatisfied in matters of love. If someone else is being buried, you will soon find out that someone close to you has fallen ill.

G

GARDEN

Contentment with your life. If you are strolling through a garden, you can expect that the complacency you are experiencing will last for a long time.

GHOST

Danger; especially if the ghost is of a deceased parent or close friend.

GLOVES

Exercise caution in your financial dealings.

GOGGLES

A key person in your life is trying to manipulate you. Do not allow yourself to be persuaded by those whom you do not fully trust.

GRAVE

A bad omen. Dreaming of a grave is said to precede a major disappointment in your life.

GYPSY

If you dream that a gypsy is reading your palm or telling your future, beware. It means that you are about to enter into a marriage or other important union that will be unsuccessful.

H

HAND

If the hand is well manicured and youthful, look forward to success. If the hand is old and wrinkled, beware of an upcoming financial disaster.

HARP

A period of bliss and merriment will soon come to an end.

HAT

Hats are associated with fortune in the business world. If you are sporting a new hat in your dream, you may be considering a lucrative business deal. If you lose your hat in your dream, it is a sign that you are headed for a work-related disaster.

HELL

Dangerous temptations.

HERMIT

To see a hermit in your dreams indicates that you have been, or will soon be, betrayed by someone close to you. If you, yourself, are the hermit, you have been a good and true friend to others—whether or not they have reciprocated your selflessness.

HERO

If you dream of being a hero, it is a sign that you should "go for it." It is time to take action and pursue your goals.

HOME

A shabby or unkempt home indicates you must take more care of your finances. A house that appears in good condition portends a period of economical comfort.

HORSE

A healthy, well-groomed horse indicates a satisfactory love life. A sick or malnourished horse suggests questions about your partner's fidelity. If a horse should buck you, a rival may be seeking to destroy your love life.

HOSPITAL

If you are in a hospital or infirmary, someone you consider a friend is out to harm you. If you are leaving a hospital, you have escaped (or soon will escape) the clutches of this hurtful person.

I

J

JAIL

If you are the person in jail, you may feel you are unqualified in some area. If another person is in jail, you may feel that someone is taking you for granted

ICE

A period of distress.

ICE CREAM

A good omen—you will have time to enjoy life's little pleasures.

INCENSE

Friends will be more supportive of you than ever before.

JEALOUSY

You are jealous of someone you know, though the person in the dream may not be the one you are jealous of.

IVY

You will enjoy good health and prosperity.

JOURNEY

If your journey is pleasant, your career is (or soon will be) on track. If the trip is not enjoyable, you may be having job-related problems.

K

KEY

Losing a key suggests domestic turmoil. If you find a key, or keys play a useful role in your dream, you can expect a lengthy period of tranquility in your household.

KISS

The person being kissed is more meaningful to you than you may have realized. If you are not physically attracted to the person you are kissing, you may envy this person or desire to be more like him or her.

KITE

If it is you who is flying the kite, you have been pretentious and a bit of a showoff of late. Should the kite drop to the ground or become entangled in a tree, you can expect to be knocked off your high horse. If, however, the kite flies so high that you lose sight of it, pleasant surprises are on the way.

KNIFE

A bad omen. You are or soon will be involved in a major dispute. The larger or rustier the knife is, the more serious the dispute will be.

KNOCKING

You will soon receive unexpected news. The louder the knocking, the more important the news.

L

LADDER

If a ladder is propped up for you to climb, it indicates future success. If you climb down from or fall from a ladder, be prepared for professional disappointment.

LAMP

A brightly lit lamp means you soon will be enlightened about something important. A dim lamp suggests that loved ones are keeping you in the dark about something significant.

LAUGHING

You are seeking a more eventful social life.

LEAKING

Something of a crucial importance to you has been lost.

LEMON

You are envious of someone you recently met.

LEPROSY

You are more upset than you realize about a recent loss.

LIFEBOAT

If you are in a lifeboat, you have given up on something rather than persevering.

LION

You are feeling driven by something forceful—that force is depicted as a lion. If the lion in your dream is in a cage, you must overcome many trails and tribulations in order to achieve the success you seek. Lion cubs signify new undertaking or ventures that will enable you to accomplish the ambitious goals you have set for yourself. A lion's roar portends unexpected advancement in your career.

LIZARD

An enemy is trying everything in his or her power to destroy you. If you manage to destroy the lizard, you will prevail in an upcoming battle. If the lizard remains at large in your dream, it is likely that your enemy will prevail.

LYING

If you are the liar in a dream, you feel guilty about the dishonorable way you have been treating someone.

M

MAP

Indicates that you want to make a significant change in your life, such as a relocation or change of job.

MASK

Duplicity. If you are wearing a mask in your dream, you may be ashamed of some aspect of your behavior.

MEDICINE

If you take medicine in the dream, a major worry will cease to be a problem for you. If, however, you dispense medicine to another, you do not wish this person well.

MILK

A life of luxury and ease.

MISTLETOE

Portends an enjoyable reunion with a close friend or lover.

MOTHER (OR MOTHER FIGURE)

If there is a maternal figure in the dream, such as a caring mother or grandmother, it is an indication that you feel safe and protected. However, a negative female figure such as an "evil stepmother" is a sign that someone you thought you could trust is really out to harm you. If you are the mother in the dream, you feel responsible for taking care of others.

MOTORCYCLE

You feel in control of your life, both personally and professionally.

MOUNTAIN

(See Climbing.)

MURDER

If you are the victim of a murder, beware of enemies. If you are the murderer in your dream, you probably feel guilty about mistreating a loved one.

N

NEST

A full bird's nest symbolizes a rewarding business matter. An empty nest may symbolize feelings of melancholy about the loss of a close friend or relative.

NIGHTINGALE

A sweetly singing nightingale indicates a peaceful home and a happy marital union.

NUDITY

Embarrassment or a feeling of vulnerability.

O

OAR

Using an oar signifies that you have been sacrificing your own happiness in order to please someone else.

OCEAN

A calm ocean indicates a peaceful life. A rough ocean indicates many obstacles to overcome.

ONION

You are envied by many. The more onions in your dream, the more envied you are. If you consume the onions in their entirety, you will be unharmed by those who are jealous of you. If the onions are growing in a garden, you can expect to be challenged by people who are envious of your wealth and happiness. Onions that are cooked portend successful and solid relationships with your coworkers.

ORCHARD

An orchard filled with sweet, ripe fruit signifies a happy love life. If the orchard is barren, or its fruits are out of season, a current relationship will fail.

ORPHAN

A tendency to put the needs of others before your own.

OWL

An owl heard calling in your dreams is believed to foretell the death of a close friend or relative. If you spot a dead owl in your dream, it means that someone you know who is sick may soon lose his or her battle with the illness. An owl seen but not heard in a tree is a warning—beware the wrath of an enemy.

P

PAIN

There is a need to consult a doctor about your health. If others are in pain, your ability to make decisions may be questionable.

PARACHUTE

A descending parachute signifies a deep desire to abandon something in your life.

PARADISE

If you're dwelling in paradise, you can count on your friends and family. If, however, you are seeking paradise but never find it, it is a sign to be careful when making decisions.

PEACOCK

You are attracted to someone who is not genuine.

PEARLS

Loss of a pearl necklace suggests your success is in jeopardy.

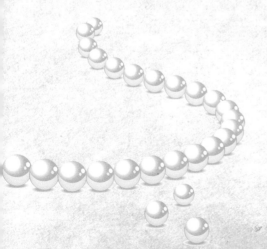

PIANO

Seeing or listening to a piano means you may be about to receive some wonderful news. If, however, the piano is broken or out of tune, the news will not be so good.

PICKPOCKET

Someone you are close to is not trustworthy.

POISON

If you have been poisoned, someone you consider to be a friend is really duplicitous. If you poison someone, it is a sign you have become jealous of a close friend.

PRIEST

A bad omen. You will soon suffer a humiliation or deception.

R

RABBIT

A white rabbit is a good omen, signifying a faithful lover or a positive event in the near future.

RACE

Stiff competition. If you win the race, you will surpass any and all opponents in your quest for professional success.

RAINBOW

A symbol of merriment and joy. Your worries will soon end and your relationships with those close to you will thrive.

RAFT

(See Boat.)

RAPIDS

Rapid "white water" signifies an incredibly stressful period in your life. If you are immersed in the rapids, it's a sign that you are in the midst of this stressful period and should seek help. If you are watching the rapids from a distance, a period of great anxiety may be coming your way.

RAZOR

Expect a major disagreement with a loved one. If the razor cuts skin, an arrangement you made with someone is about to fall through. A razor that is broken or rusty portends distress and disappointment.

RECORD PLAYER

You can expect many years of joy and family harmony.

RICE

A sign that you have a happy marriage.

RING

If you are the recipient of a ring, someone is genuinely devoted to you. If you should break or lose a ring in your dream, someone with whom you have been intimate is losing interest in you.

ROCKET

Symbol of disappointment or that you sense the time has come to make some major changes in your life.

ROCKING CHAIR

Sitting in a rocking chair indicates feelings of instability.

ROOF

Being on a rooftop indicates your career has reached or soon will reach great heights.

ROSE

An unexpected joyous occasion. However, if the roses in your dreams are withered, you may experience the loss of someone close to you. White roses generally are associated with illness—either your own or that of a loved one.

ROWBOAT

Riding in a rowboat signifies an active social life, but if the boat capsizes, expect a business failure that will lead to financial disaster.

RUNNING FOR ONE'S LIFE

A sign that you are afraid of someone or something. Another interpretation is that a woman who dreams of being chased wishes to be pursued by a suitor.

S

SATAN

(See Devil.)

SAW

Operating a saw symbolizes that your home life is improving. But if the saw is rusty or broken, you may not be able to solve some family problems.

SCISSORS

A bad omen. Generally, any dream involving scissors is associated with distrust in love affairs and marriages.

SCORPION

Danger. You have been involved in something scandalous that is close to erupting. If you are able to kill the scorpion in your dream, you will escape blame when the scandal is exposed.

SEX

Satisfying and pleasing sex indicates you are enjoying healthy relationships—whether with friends or a lover. If the sex in your dream is not fulfilling there may be problems in a relationship. If you dream of watching others having sex, you need to form new relationships.

SHEEP

Associated with a successful career. The woollier the sheep, the more potential for success.

SICKNESS

Someone in your immediate family is in jeopardy. If you are sick in your dream, you may wish to examine your behavior—you may feel guilty about something you have been feeling, thinking, or doing.

SKELETON

Ill health—you may wish to consult a doctor or strive for a healthier lifestyle. If you are the skeleton in your dreams, you have been agonizing over something that is not really of great importance.

SLEEP

Sleeping in a clean and comfortable bed means you are feeling at peace. If the bed is old, broken, or has dirty sheets, consider making some changes in your lifestyle.

SLIDING OR SLIPPING

You will experience a major disappointment. This disappointment may manifest itself in a failed love affair or a business disaster.

SNAKES

If you are bitten by a snake, you will lose an important professional battle. If you kill the snake, you will succeed in a major struggle.

SNOW

You have been worrying unnecessarily about something.

SPACE

Dreams of outer space portend a break from a restrictive lifestyle to one that you find more liberating.

SPIDER

Careful and well-planned decisions are about to pay off.

SPLINTER

Splinters signify that you are envied by someone you consider a rival.

SQUIRREL

Who doesn't look forward to a visit from friends? Well, friends will soon be on the their way to see you. If you happen to injure (accidentally or on purpose) a squirrel, you are in danger of losing a friend. If you dream of petting a squirrel, you and your family can expect years of joy.

STAIRS

Ascending a staircase signifies a path to personal and professional success. If you are descending or falling down the stairs, the path on which you are headed will take a sudden and unfortunate turn.

STALLION

Seeing a stallion or riding one portends a life of affluence and accomplishments.

STEALING

If you are stealing something, it's a sign that you should re-evaluate the way you have been treating others.

SUBWAY

Emotional distress.

SUN

If the sun is rising, you will soon accomplish great things. Seeing the sun at high noon means you are at a wonderful stage in your life. If the sun is setting, it is a sign you should guard your possessions carefully.

SWAMP

A rocky relationship will soon end.

SWIMMING

You are prepared for an important career change or a relocation.

T

TABLE

A table that is set with food and silverware means you will be reunited with a long-lost loved one. If the table is empty, you will experience a period of loneliness and distress.

TAPEWORM

A warning that you will soon find yourself battling a healthy problem.

TEETH

Usually a sign of illness.

TELEPHONE

Hearing a telephone ring or speaking on a phone means you will soon meet a stranger who will have a major impact on your life.

TICKLE

Being tickled may indicate you have an undiagnosed illness. If you are the tickler in the dream, you may be at risk of losing something valuable due to indiscretion or thoughtlessness.

TORNADO

A recent business decision was unwise.

TRAIN

You will soon need to make an unexpected trip. If the ride is quick and pleasant in your dream, your journey will be rewarding. If the train is crowded and the trip arduous, it would be wise to avoid any travel in the near future.

TRAMPOLINE

You have been on an emotional roller coaster lately. This ride is about to end. It is important to recall how you felt while you jumped on the trampoline. If you enjoyed the experience, you will find that your recent up-and-down feelings will end in a positive way. If, however, jumping on the trampoline was an unpleasant experience, you may find yourself disappointed at the end of your struggles.

TUNNEL

Entering a tunnel means you will soon experience a major loss—either in your personal or professional life. Seeing a train in the tunnel indicates a period of grave illness.

TURKEY

There will be a major turn in your career. You can expect financial woes to cease and prosperity to ensue. If the turkeys are ill (or dead), your pride will be diminished by an upcoming business squabble. If the turkeys are in flight, you can expect your fiscal status to take a major turn for the better.

U V

UMBRELLA

Carrying an umbrella in the rain signifies that you are experiencing a frustrating period in your life. If you are carrying an umbrella and it is not raining, it is a sign that you are accustomed to nuisances.

VALENTINE

Writing or sending valentines may mean you have recently developed feelings for a close friend that are stronger than you had realized.

VAMPIRE

Beware. Someone with whom you have recently become involved does not have your best interest in mind.

VASE

A vase filled with flowers portends a contented domestic life. If the vase is empty, your hopes for such a life will take more work than you had formerly realized.

VEIL

Wearing a veil may mean you have been unfaithful to your lover—either in thought or deed. If the veil is lifted, your infidelity will soon be discovered.

VINES

Expect a long period of prosperity.

VIOLIN

A good omen, indicating peace and love at home.

VOLCANO

Involvement in a harmful relationship that is characterized by jealously and greed.

VULTURE

Beware of someone who may bring you harm. If you kill the vulture in your dream, you will escape the clutches of your enemy.

W

WAGON

If the wagon is a covered one, your family will be plagued by many problems, and you will be the one most affected.

WALKING STICK

You have been, or will soon become, dependent upon others.

WASP

If you see a wasp or are stung by one, it is likely that someone is trying to manipulate you. If you kill the wasp, it is a sign you will manage to rid this person from your life.

WHEEL

The more quickly the wheel is spinning, the sooner you will achieve success. If the wheel is broken, you will find it difficult to achieve your goals.

WHISTLE

Hearing a whistle blow means that upsetting news will soon interrupt a pleasant period in your life. If, in your dream, you are blowing a whistle, you will make a sudden and significant change in your life.

WINDOW

Open windows signify that you are responsive to your surroundings. You are feeling optimistic and open-minded about things that are new and foreign to you. If, however, the windows are closed or you are seeking to close them, you may be restricted by old habits that are not necessarily going to serve you well in the future.

WINGS

You are consumed with worry for a loved one who has recently moved.

WORMS

You will soon be in a position where you must associate with people you do not like. If the worms are used as bait in your dream, you will be able to keep your professional distance from these people while maintaining your tact.

Y

YARDSTICK

Anxiety. Eliminate the things that are causing you the most stress and direct your energy towards what is truly important to you.